HOUDINI'S CARD TRICKS

TEACH YOURSELF THE TRICKS OF THE WORLD'S MOST FAMOUS MAGICIAN

BY

J. C. CANNELL

Copyright © 2013 Read Books Ltd.
This book is copyright and may not be
reproduced or copied in any way without
the express permission of the publisher in writing

British Library Cataloguing-in-Publication Data
A catalogue record for this book is available from the
British Library

CONTENTS

Card Manipulation

Card manipulation is the branch of magical illusion that deals with creating effects using sleight of hand techniques involving playing cards. Card manipulation is often used in magical performances, to great effect, especially in close-up, parlour and street magic. Some of the most recognised names in this field include Dai Vernon, a Canadian magician with considerable influence, specialising in sleight of hand, Ed Marlo, an American born magician who referred to himself as a 'cardician', and Alex Elmsley, a Scot who was notable for his invention of the Ghost Count or Elmsley Count, creating various mathematical card tricks, and for publishing the mathematics of card shuffling. Before becoming world famous for his escapology act, Houdini billed himself as 'The King of Cards'.

Cards have a long and illustrious history, they were first invented in Imperial China, and specimens have been found dating back as early the ninth century, during the Tang Dynasty (618-907). Female players were some of the most frequent participants, and the first known book on cards, called Yezi Gexi (presumably written in the 860s) was originally written by a Tang era woman, subsequently undergoing additions by other Chinese scholars. By the eleventh century, playing cards could be found throughout the Asian continent. During the Ming Dynasty (1368–1644), characters from novels such as the Water Margin were widely featured on the faces of playing cards. Playing cards first entered Europe in the early fourteenth century, probably from Egypt, with suits (sets of cards with matching designs) very similar to the tarot suits of Swords, Staves, Cups and Coins (also known as disks or pentacles). These latter markings are still used in traditional Italian, Spanish and Portuguese decks. Playing cards were first formalised into something closely resembling our modern deck in the seventeenth century, but the joker was only introduced by the USA in the 1870s.

As props, playing cards have only become popular with magicians in the last century or so, largely due to their inexpensive nature, versatility and easy availability. Although magicians have created and presented myriad of illusions with cards (sometimes referred to as tricks), most of these illusions are generally considered to be built upon one hundred or so basic principles and techniques. Presentation and context (including patter, the conjurer's misleading account of what he is doing) account for many of the variations. Card magic, in one form or another, likely dates from the time playing cards became commonly known, towards the second half of the fourteenth century, but its history in this period is largely undocumented. Compared to sleight of hand magic in general and to cups and balls, it is a relatively new form of magic. Common manipulation techniques include 'lifts', where one or more cards (normally known to the audience) are selected and identified as part of the illusion, 'false deals', which appear to deliver cards fairly, when actually the cards are predetermined or known to the performer, and 'side slips', a technique generally used to bring a predetermined card to the top of a deck. Passes, Palming, False Shuffles, False Cuts, Changes, Crimps, Jogs and Reverses are also commonly utilised manipulations.

CARD TRICKS

EXAMPLES OF THOUGHT-READING—A CODE—
THE JUMPING CARDS—MAGNETIC ACES—THE
CHANGEOVER—A FEAT OF STRENGTH—THE
BOOMERANG CARD—CUTTING THE CARDS—
THE TORN CARD—VANISHING CARDS BY
PISTOL—THE FOUR ACES—THE HERSCHELL
CARD-STABBING TRICK

AS Houdini in the early part of his career was known as the
"Card King," this book would be incomplete if it did not
contain some of his tricks with cards. I have had to select from
some hundreds, but I have given in simple language those
which can be understood by the ordinary reader. With the
exception of one or two which involve the "pass" of the expert,
most of these tricks can be reproduced by the competent
amateur.

Reasonably simple tricks are here given, together with
those of an advanced type. Here is one in which a telephone
figures:

Show six cards and ask someone in your audience to think
of any one of the six and to name the card. Next request him
to go to the telephone and ring up a number which you give

him, to ask for a Mr. ——. "What card have I just selected, Mr. ——?" is the question to be asked. The person thus rung up will reply correctly to the question.

And this is how it is done. The man at the other end of the telephone is an accomplice, of course. The names of the six cards to be used in the trick have been written down by him, and against each one is written the name of a person. Thus, against the first card is written a name beginning with "A." Against the second card is written a name beginning with "B," and so on with the remaining four cards. The conjurer remembers the names and the cards.

All he has to do, therefore, when he knows the card which his assistant has selected, is to ask him to ring up the number and ask for Mr. ——, filling in the name given to that particular card.

His accomplice knows, directly he hears the name, which card is being thought of.

A medium or confederate is necessary in the method here described.

The conjurer asks someone to take three consecutive cards from a pack, which has really been prearranged in a certain order, and to place them in a row on the table. He says it is quite impossible for him to know the cards, but he will look at them, think of them, and then "transfer his thoughts" to the medium sitting at the other end of the room beyond and behind the audience. So that the medium will not be suspected of looking for signals he turns his back on the performer during the process of "thought-transference." The medium names the cards correctly.

This is the explanation: directly the chosen cards are taken away the magician holds quite casually the top half of the pack, from the bottom of which the cards have been selected, with its face towards the audience, and the medium sees the bottom card. Knowing the order of the cards, the medium can then tell at once which three cards are on the table. By that time, as the medium has memorised the pack by means of a code, he knows which cards must follow the bottom one shown to him by the performer. Those are the three cards taken away by the member of the audience. Here is the code-sentence which enables the pack to be memorised—Eight kings threatened to save nine fair ladies for one sick knave.

The pack should be arranged in the order: diamonds, spades, hearts, clubs.

The interpretation of the code is—Eight (eight)—kings (King)—threatened (three, ten)—to (two)—save (seven)—nine (nine)—fair (five)—ladies (Queen)—for (four)—one (Ace)—sick (six)—knave (Jack).

By memorising this sentence, and remembering the order of the different suits in the pack, the code is made easy, if the cards are previously arranged in their correct positions.

Many tricks can be done by means of this code.

Taking six cards from the pack, the magician asks someone to think of one of them and then to replace the cards.

Dealing the cards in small lots of five or six the conjurer asks the spectator, as he does so, if he can see the card of which he is thinking. Directly the answer "Yes" is given the conjurer names the card.

In this case, when the six cards are returned to the pack the conjurer slips his little finger under all of them, and, by means of the pass, brings the lot to the bottom of the pack. He then shuffles the cards, taking care not to disturb those at the bottom of the pack, and immediately afterwards deals a few cards and includes in the lot one of those from the bottom of the pack. Thus, in each lot he exposes there will always be one of the six cards which the spectator took, and this one will be the bottom card. Therefore, directly the conjurer is told that the card of which the spectator is thinking is visible he knows at once which card it is, and names it.

In this "thought-reading" trick, the conjurer comes forward with a new pack of cards. He calls attention to the fact that the Government stamp is on the wrapper before he breaks open the pack, and holds out the cards, first to one spectator and then another, until about a dozen cards have been chosen. When the required number of cards have been selected, the conjurer hands the pack to each person who has taken a card, and asks him to return it himself and to shuffle the cards. When all the cards have been returned to the pack, the magician asks those who took cards to think of them, and then he tells them of what cards they are thinking.

Let me point out again that the pack of cards is a new one, and that it is not tampered with in any way before it is opened.

The secret is that cards belonging to one particular "brand" are packed in the same way. Open any pack of Steamboats—these are made especially for conjuring, though they look like ordinary cards—and you will find that the cards are packed in this order: Spades 2–10; Diamonds 2–10; Hearts 2–7, and Ace, King, Queen, Jack; Diamonds, King, Queen, Jack, Ace; Spades, Ace, King, Queen, Jack; Clubs, King, Queen Jack, Ace; Hearts 8–10; Clubs 2–10.

This order must be committed to memory, but it is not a difficult task to do this.

To discover the chosen card one must, while walking away to another member of the audience, turn up with the left thumb the corner of the card immediately above that which was taken.

It will be noted that the magician does not have each card returned immediately after it has been taken away.

If the man selecting a card were given the opportunity to

replace it at once, he might upset the order of the cards.

The services of a confederate are required for this card trick which will baffle most people.

In the temporary absence of the performer, a card is selected from a pack and shown to the members of the audience. When he returns to the room, he names the chosen card.

And this is how it's done: before the trick starts the confederate lights a cigarette and stands behind the others, apparently engaged only in watching and smoking, but is actually giving signals to the performer.

The performer should place his hand to his forehead as if "to control his thoughts," but really to get a chance of observing his confederate's signals.

The code is as follows: if the card is an ace, the cigarette is held in the right hand by the thumb and first finger. If a two, it is held in the same hand by the thumb and second finger; if a three, the same hand and third finger; if a four, the same hand by thumb and little finger; if a five, the same hand by thumb and first two fingers; if a six, the same hand by thumb and two middle fingers; if a seven, the same hand by thumb, third and little finger; if eight, the same hand by thumb and all the fingers; if a nine, it is held left hand by thumb and first finger; if a ten, in the left hand by thumb and second finger; if a knave, in the left hand by thumb and third finger; if a queen, in the left hand by thumb and first two fingers; if a king, in the left hand by thumb and all the fingers. To give the different suits, the cigarette is placed or held as follows: clubs, put the cigarette in the right-hand corner of the mouth; hearts, place the cigarette in the left-hand corner of the mouth; spades, have the cigarette in the middle of the mouth; diamonds, hold it away from the mouth.

To perform the trick of making a card "jump," show the top card of the pack and place it in the centre. Command it to jump back to its former place on the top, and ask anyone to prove that it has not obeyed your command.

This is how it is done: the top card of the pack is the eight of clubs; the second card is the seven of clubs. Take off these two cards and show them as one; then put them back on top of the pack. Take off the top card (the eight of clubs) and place it slowly in the centre of the pack. When it is half-way into the pack show the face of it to the audience, who, seeing the top half, believe that it is really the seven of clubs. But you must be sure and keep your hand over the index number in the corner.

MAGNETIC ACES

It is easy to mystify an audience with this trick. The conjurer takes the ace of diamonds, the ace of clubs and the ace of spades from the pack and holds them towards the audience with the ace of diamonds in the centre and the other two cards diagonally across it, so that only the top of the red ace is seen. The conjurer then takes one of the black aces and openly places it at the bottom of the pack. The other black ace is laid on the top of the pack, and then the conjurer takes the remaining ace and puts it in the centre of the pack. To convince the audience that everything so far has been quite fair he shows the top and bottom cards once more. Everyone sees that they are the two black aces.

"Now," says the conjurer, "we will place one black ace in the centre of the pack and another a few cards away." He puts both aces in the centre of the pack. Then he continues, "We have all three aces—the ace of clubs, the ace of spades and the ace of diamonds—in the centre of the pack. Ace of diamonds—jump!"

He taps the top of the pack and asks someone to take off the top card. It is the ace of diamonds. Someone is sure to suggest that there must be more than one ace of diamonds in the pack, whereupon the conjurer hands the pack out for inspection and anyone can prove to the satisfaction of the audience that the pack contains only the usual number of aces.

It is so easily explained. The trick is brought about solely by the manner in which the cards are held in the first place, and by a little subterfuge. In running through the cards with the object of taking out the three aces the conjurer secretly pushes the ace of diamonds on to the top of the pack and takes from it the ace of hearts and the two black aces. He places the two black aces over the ace of hearts so that only the point of the heart is visible. The ace of hearts then appears to be the ace of diamonds. After the conjurer has put the two black aces in the centre of the pack he has really finished the trick, and the rest is showmanship.

THE CHANGE OVER

In this trick, the ability to palm cards is necessary. The performer takes the two red cards of any number, say the ten of hearts and ten of diamonds, and places them under a handkerchief on the table. He puts the two black tens under another handkerchief. He then commands them to change places, and lifting the handkerchief, shows that his "command" has been "obeyed."

It is done in this way. The conjurer has two extra black tens in his right-hand trousers pocket. In taking out the two handkerchiefs to be used in the trick he palms these cards. Picking up the two red tens, he covers them with the palmed black ones and shows the two red ones. The audience are unaware of the presence of the two black ones behind the red ones. In covering these with a large handkerchief the conjurer palms away the two red ones, but as the audience see the shape of the remaining two cards under the handkerchief they believe they are the same two cards they have just seen—the red ones. In picking up the two black tens, the magician palms the two red ones on top of them and squaring the cards shows the face of the front black ten. The audience believe that only the two black cards are there. In covering these with the second handkerchief the conjurer palms away the two black tens and leaves the two red ones under the handkerchief. He slips the two palmed cards into a pocket and commands the cards to "change over."

Here is another trick in which the conjurer has three or four cards selected and returned to the pack. Taking the pack in his left hand, and showing his right hand empty, he throws the cards into the air, and while they are falling catches at some of them with his right hand. When the other cards have dropped the conjurer is seen to be holding the cards that were selected and returned to the pack.

It will require practice to do this. When the cards are returned the conjurer brings them to the top of the pack by means of the pass, and turning a little to his right, palms them off the pack and then back-palms them. The selected cards are now at the back of the right hand, which can then be shown with the palm towards the audience. The conjurer throws up the pack with his left hand and in putting his right hand among the falling cards brings those which were palmed to view again.

Another variation of the trick is that the magician has two cards selected and returned to the pack. He then throws the whole pack into the air, quickly plunges his hand among the falling cards, and catches two cards, which are found to be the two cards which were selected.

In this case, the two cards were brought to the top of the pack by means of the pass and then one of them was shuffled to the bottom of the pack. The conjurer held the pack with his thumb in the middle of one side and his fingers in the middle of the other. In throwing up the pack the top and bottom cards were thus drawn away from the rest and all that the conjurer had to do was to grip them tightly while he placed his hand among the falling cards.

A FEAT OF STRENGTH

To tear a pack of cards in half hold them by putting the right hand over one end of the pack and the left hand under the opposite end with the fingers on the opposite side.

Now the pack can be held tightly between the two hands and by suddenly twisting the two hands—the right hand towards him and the left hand away from him—the conjurer contrives to tear the pack. Cheap cards are the easiest to tear.

Here is the boomerang trick: the conjurer throws a card

away from him and causes it to return to his hand; as it comes back he picks up a pair of scissors and, catching the card with them, cuts it in halves.

To do this the magician holds the card between the second finger and thumb, with the first finger curled over the top corner. He then bends the hand inwards so that the card nearly touches the wrist, and in throwing the card away from him jerks it back by means of the first finger on the corner. The card is thrown away, but is revolving on its own axis all the time, and this motion causes it to return to the thrower.

To indicate red or black cards as requested by his audience, the magician begins by having all the black cards at the top of the pack and all the red ones together underneath. Slipping his little finger in the pack between the two sets, he is able to insert his middle finger. Then, using the right hand, he bends all the cards below the middle finger in the opposite direction. The cards can then be shuffled, but when they are spread on the table all the black ones will be slightly convex and all the red ones slightly concave. A new pack should be used, and only a very slight bend in the cards is necessary.

IN THE DARK

The performer requests the person taking a card to show it to someone else, so there may be no doubt afterwards as to which card was taken. He then explains that he is going to perform the trick in the dark, that is to say, the cards are going to be in the "dark."

He squares up the pack and asks the person who has taken the card to place it in the centre of the pack. The conjurer then puts the cards in the "dark" by covering them with a handkerchief and placing them on the table. Directly he has done so he asks the person who took the card to think of it, and the conjurer at once names the card.

This is the secret: when the card is being shown to the second person, the conjurer has ample time to make the necessary move for the accomplishment of the trick. He turns over the bottom card of the pack so that when he squares up the cards and holds them with the bottom card upwards, the cards appear to be all face downwards in the usual way. When the card is returned all that the conjurer has to do is to turn over the pack once more and spread out the cards on the table while he is covering them with a handkerchief. He is then able to see the chosen card through the handkerchief because that card is facing him.

Having asked someone to cut the pack and to remember the card at which he made the cut, the performer picks up the cards and, running them over, at once names the card at which the person looked.

How is it done? Well, few persons ever replace the cards properly. It will be found that most people replace the portion they lift off in such a way that the cards are not quite level. In other words, they leave what is known as a "step." In picking up the cards the conjurer presses down on the pack with his first finger so as not to shift the cards at the step, and he is then able to discover exactly where the pack was cut.

A TORN CARD TRICE

A woman in the audience is asked to name any card she likes, and upon her doing so the performer finds it in the pack and gives it to her with a request to tear it up. This being done, one corner is retained and the remaining pieces "vanished" or burnt, and upon the card being reproduced minus one corner the retained piece exactly fits.

The following apparatus is needed: a "magic" pistol, a plate, three packs of thin cards, exactly alike, a small frame, and a small cap of stiff black paper to fit over one corner of a card giving the appearance of the corner being missing when held against a black coat.

The pistol, frame and plate are on the table and the corner fake in a convenient pocket. One pack is arranged in a known order so that a given card may be instantly found. This packet is concealed in a small pocket behind the left hip with one end protruding so as to be easily pulled out. The other two packs are arranged as one big pack in regular order, each suit separately, and every duplicate card together, i.e. 2, 2; 3, 3; 4, 4; 5, 5; 6, 6; 7, 7; 8, 8; 9, 9; 10, 10; Kn, Kn; Q, Q; K, K; Ace, Ace. The performer comes forward with a double pack in his hand, taking care to hold it so that the extra thickness is not noticeable. The thinnest cards are, of course, the best for this trick.

Supposing the woman selects the four of diamonds, he runs through the pack until he comes to the two cards of that name. He then takes one out and hands it to her, slipping his little finger under the other one (cards are face upwards); the "pass" is then made and the pack turned back upwards, this bringing the duplicate four of diamonds to the top, and while instructing the woman how to tear up the card she has, he tears one of the lower corners off the top card and palms it in the right hand. This is a simple move, as all eyes are on the woman's card. The fingers of the hand holding the pack must close over it so as to hide the missing corner. The performer picks up the plate from the table with the left hand (which holds the pack) and asks the woman to place the pieces on it. He then selects one corner (really the palmed one) and gives it to her and carries the plate back to the table in his right hand. Under cover of putting the plate down (right side to audience) he drops the double pack (except the top card, the four of diamonds) into his "profonde" and obtains the other arranged pack, which he places on the table, retaining the four of diamonds with the corner off in his palm. This sounds difficult, but will be understood better if the performer palms the card off before changing the packs. The palmed card does not interfere with the change.

He then picks up the frame and takes the back out, handing the whole thing for examination. While this is being done he obtains the loan of a handkerchief, and asking permission of the woman who selected the card originally, he spreads it on her lap. Then obtaining possession of the frame he puts the back on, at the same time slipping the palmed card in, and placing it face downwards on the handkerchief, asks the woman to wrap it up by folding the four corners inward. The performer loads the pieces of card into his pistol from the plate and fires in the air, and the woman finds the card in the frame, testifying to the corner fitting exactly. While attention is fixed on the woman, the performer picks up the pack from the table, and in accordance with his memorised system, makes the pass at the nearest point and gets the four of diamonds to the top. Dropping his hand to his pocket, he obtains the black corner, slips it on the card and keeps it concealed with his fingers. By this time the woman will have finished her part of the trick by seeing that the corner fits. It is now that the card is changed for the duplicate with the fake. Taking the card in his right hand, he also picks up the handkerchief with the same hand and places the latter in his left, which holds the pack. At the moment the hands are together, the card is changed for the one on the pack, keeping the black corner concealed by the fingers. The handkerchief is then handed to the owner. Turning again to the woman, the performer asks for the missing corner, holding out a card as a kind of tray for her to put it on. Holding them at arm's length he walks back to the table ostensibly to place the pack down, but really to get sufficiently far from the spectators to show the card (with the fake) against his coat, which, of course, everyone takes to be the same card as the woman had. All he has to do now is to palm the loose corner and fake under pretence of running the card and piece together and getting rid of them into his "profonde" as he advances to have the card examined.

VANISHING CARDS BY PISTOL

The effect is that three envelopes are sealed by the audience, one inside the other, the outer one being strung upon a tape, which is tied between two brass pillars, fitted into the table. A small silk handkerchief is now covered over the envelope. A card selected from the pack is deprived of one corner, which is retained by the audience; the card is placed on top of the pistol in full view of the audience, yet it vanishes immediately upon the pistol being fired, and the effect of the shot is not only to vanish the card, but the handkerchief over the envelope.

The envelope is next cut down and slit open, and the second one taken out; this is in turn opened, and the smaller one given, still sealed, to the audience, who, upon opening it, discover the card minus the corner inside. On the corner which was retained being fitted to the card, it proves to be an exact fit.

The explanation lies firstly in the pistol, which, although apparently quite innocent, has really a coiled spring fitted inside the barrel around the centre tube; this is in turn enclosed in another split barrel, which has a cogged end. This tube has four steel pins brazed in the open split pointing towards the opposite direction in which the spring is wound.

To set the pistol, the barrel is twisted to its full extent, and a lever pushed down to keep it from revolving. When the hammer is cocked all is ready, as it follows that if a card is placed in the slit, the hammer, upon the pistol being fired, strikes the lever which releases the cogs, causing the inside barrel to revolve rapidly, the pins catching the card and rolling it round inside the outer case. So much for the vanishing of the card.

The next things to be considered are the envelopes. These are unprepared and are really fastened by the audience, but unknown to them, the tablecloth has a small slit large enough to take an envelope the same size as the smaller of the three, and contains a card similar to that selected by the audience, but minus a corner. Upon receiving the envelopes back, the performer lays them on the table casually over the slit; this enables him to pick up the concealed one with the three, a small piece of wax causing it to adhere to the back of the envelopes. He hangs the collection up by the tape after exhibiting the pillars, and covers over the lot with a handkerchief which is fastened by a thread to the centre, and is vanished down the table leg by means of a thread and weight.

To open the envelopes it is necessary only to cut the tapes, and with the scissors slip open the first envelope along the top, the forefinger and thumb withdrawing the envelope inside and at the same time the one outside. The second envelope is now opened in the same way, but this time, instead of drawing out the inside envelope, the duplicate containing the card is apparently taken out and handed to the audience to open, the other envelope being left inside. No one ever thinks of asking to look into the second envelope, or suspects that the exhibited one does not really come from inside. The "corner trick" is performed when replacing the cards upon the table after the selection.

THE DEVO CARD TRICK

For this the performer has the assistance of two men from the audience.

They are handed an ordinary pack of cards, with a request to remove the four aces and four kings from the pack, and, if they desire, privately to mark them with a pencil. Two ordinary envelopes are also examined, and on one they write "Aces," on the other "Kings." The performer calls for the envelope on which "Aces" has been written, placing the aces in full view inside the envelope, and giving it in charge of one of the men. In like manner, he places the kings in the other envelope, which is held by the second man.

The marked aces and kings change places from one envelope to the other!

Take a duplicate ace of hearts and a duplicate king of diamonds, fake these cards by colouring their backs the same as your table-top, preferably a dead black. Have these faked cards lying face downwards on the table-top, where they will be invisible by reason of the faked backs. You are also provided with an ordinary pack of cards, two ordinary envelopes and a lead pencil. Obtain the assistance of two men; hand them the pack with a request to remove the four aces and kings and mark them as already indicated.

While the examination of the envelopes is in progress, take back the aces first by showing the cards, then shuffle, and toy with them. If the ace of hearts is not already in front bring it there. In the same manner take back kings; see that the king of diamonds is in front. Place the packet of four aces down over your fake king of diamonds and your packet of kings over the fake ace of hearts, showing your hands entirely empty.

Now call for the envelope on which "Aces" is written; take up from table apparently the four aces, really the kings, with fake ace in front; the audience seeing the front card unchanged do not suspect a change has been made. Take the envelope and, turning cards with backs to spectators (after showing them) appear to place them in it. In reality the four kings go inside the envelope, the fake ace is allowed to slide down behind it, held by thumb of hand holding envelope; in the act of raising the envelope to lips to seal flap (a natural movement) the fake ace is palmed in left hand. Give envelope back to the men, getting rid of the palmed fake card meanwhile. Now pick up (apparently) the packet of kings (really aces with faked king in front) and repeat the movements as above.

ANOTHER CARD TRICK

Requisites: spirit-writing slate; plain frame with clear glass front and loose back fastened in with cross-bar; forcing pack; photographs of three statesmen pasted on back of three cards to match forcing pack; and paper bag made double—really two bags fastened together.

Effect.—The freely selected cards leave a marked envelope held by one of the audience, and appear in the empty frame. The names of three cards are found written on two slates. In place of the cards, the envelope contains three photographs of statesmen, whose names are found written on a piece of paper which has been freely selected out of a dozen or more collected from the audience, after they have written on them the names of any three statesmen.

Secret.—Arrange forcing pack as follows: suppose it is composed of ace, ten and three, put a ten, then a three, then an ace and so on through the pack. Offer the pack to be cut, and have the three top cards taken, when they are bound to take the three cards you wish to force. Have them shown to the audience and put in the envelope. Take the envelope, and, in walking back to the stage, change it; then, as if you had forgotten, say you will have it marked (they will then, of course, mark the changed envelope, which contains the three photos). Leave it with the audience. Next give out a number of slips of paper for them to write on the names of the three statesmen. Collect them in bag, double bag, one side containing several slips, all having written on them the names of the three statesmen you have in the envelope. In walking back, turn bag around, and ask someone freely to select any paper he chooses—all being alike he cannot take the wrong one—and retain it. Now show slate, on which you have beforehand written the names of the three cards you forced, and covered up with loose flap—blank at both sides—and put it down on the table. Next call attention to the frame, which you take to pieces. Take out the back, then the brown paper, which now has the cards underneath, without turning it over (cards will now face the glass), and put in the back. Fasten all up in the handkerchief, without letting the audience see the front of the frame, or they will see the cards there, and give it to someone to hold. Command the changes to take place, and show the slate with the names of the cards written on frame, with the three cards in, and the envelope will contain the three photos of the statesmen whose names are written on the slip of paper.

THE THOUGHT-READER'S BOX

Having shuffled a pack of cards, the conjurer places it in a little wooden box, into which it exactly fits, and closes the lid. He asks someone to mention a small number under 10. Suppose the number is "five."

"Very well," says the conjurer, "we shall deal with the five top cards of the pack in the box. Will you please take the box from the table and give it to me?"

The performer then names the five top cards and removes them one at a time, as he names them. The box can be thoroughly examined, and the cards are, of course, above suspicion.

The trick is done in the following manner: the lid of the box is almost as deep as the box itself and is ornamented with a small black disc of wood in the centre. This little black disc is there for a purpose. When the conjurer opens the box, the audience see that the disc in the lid goes right through it—or apparently goes right through it. As a matter of fact the disc seen in the inside of the lid is not the one in the lid itself. It is the disc in a thin wooden flap fitting snugly, but not tightly, in the lid. Behind that flap are ten cards, with their faces towards the flap. Therefore, when the box is closed and the flap falls down on to the pack, the ten cards fall with it, and as the side of the flap which is then uppermost is covered with the back of a card, it passes as a card. The pack with the fake in it can be taken out of the box and the box can be given for examination. Of course, the conjurer must know the top ten cards by heart and in their right order.

THE TWEEZERS TRICE

Having shuffled a pack of cards, the magician lifts off about half of them and gives the cards to a member of the audience. Requesting that he will select three of the cards and return the remainder, the conjurer turns his back on the audience while the person holds up the three selected cards. The conjurer then turns round, hands back the remainder of the pack to the person who chose the three cards, and asks him to shuffle the cards. The performer calls attention to the fact that during the whole progress of the trick he does not once touch the selected cards himself.

The cards are spread out, face upwards, on a tray, and the conjurer, holding a pair of small tweezers, asks the person who selected the cards to touch his wrist. He then picks up the selected cards, one at a time, with the tweezers.

It is done in this way. The shuffle is a false one. The conjurer does not disturb the top half of the pack. After three of these cards have been selected the conjurer turns his back on the audience (for the reason given above) and quietly drops the cards into his "profonde" and takes out some other cards, all of which are different from those first shown. Thus, when the cards are spread out on a tray no duplicates are visible. These cards have the white portion of their faces slightly tinged with yellow.

To get them this colour, spread the cards out to the light for a day or two. The rest is easy, because the conjurer can distinguish the chosen cards by the fact that they are slightly different in colour from the rest, being a dead white.

FOUR-ACE TRICK

The four aces are shown and laid on the table. Three cards are dealt out behind each ace. The aces are placed on the packets of three cards. A packet is chosen by the audience and placed on one side. The other three packets are turned over and the cards dealt out. The aces have disappeared. All four aces are found together in the packet chosen by the audience.

This is the way in which it is done: the first three packets of three cards are in reality packets of four cards. This is easily managed. The top two cards are taken off the pack together and shown as one card. As each card is dealt, its face is shown to the audience. When three packets have been dealt, the conjurer deals three cards which, unknown to the audience, are three duplicate aces; that is to say, these aces and the one behind which they are placed make up the four aces. These duplicate aces are, of course, dealt face downwards, but as the audience have seen the faces of the cards in the first three packets they are not likely to question this move. In squaring up each of the first three packets the conjurer contrives to get a little bit of wax from under his finger-nail on to the tops of the cards. He then covers each packet with an ace, and in doing so presses down on the first three aces. The fourth packet is then forced on the audience. The other three packets are dealt out face downwards, and as the aces adhere to the cards over which they were placed, they are "missing." The other packet is then turned over.

SEEING THE CARD

Effect.—A spectator takes a card, returns it and shuffles the pack. The conjurer spreads the cards out in a line on the table and announces that the spectator is unable to see his card. The spectator admits that he cannot see it. The conjurer picks up the cards, shuffles them, and spreads them out again. "Now," says he, "you can see your card, can't you?" The spectator admits that he can. The conjurer immediately gathers up the cards, squares up the pack, tells the spectator the name of his card and the position of it in the pack, counting from the top. The spectator is invited to count the cards and to see if the statement is correct.

Explanation.—The conjurer brings the card to the top of the pack and pushing it down with his thumb gets a glimpse at the index. He then knows the card. In spreading out the cards in a line so that they overlap one another, he takes care to hide the top card under the others. In picking up the cards and shuffling them, the magician takes off the bottom half, and in the act of shuffling some of them on the top of the others counts the cards he shuffles on the top by drawing them off one at a time with his left thumb. Then when he exposes the cards again, he can easily reckon which was the chosen one and he knows its position in the pack.

ANOTHER CHOICE

A new pack of cards is taken by the conjurer, who breaks open the wrapper, gives out the cards for examination, and asks anyone to shuffle them.

Having had the cards shuffled by the audience, the

performer invites someone to take a card and to replace it in the pack. He then shuffles the pack, and shows that the card chosen is neither at the top nor at the bottom of the pack. He produces the chosen card in any way he pleases. Perhaps the most effective way of doing this is to spread out the cards in the hands, and ask the person who chooses a card to think of it directly he sees it. After a few moments the conjurer immediately names the card.

The secret for the trick consists in one faked card. It has a small crescent-shaped piece cut out of one end. This card can easily be added to the others when the conjurer receives the pack back from the audience. The faked card is kept at first at the bottom of the pack. After a card has been chosen, the conjurer gets it to the middle of the pack, and has the chosen card placed on the top of it. The pack is then squared up.

A FAKED CARD

Holding the pack in the left hand, and lightly covering it with his right, the conjurer "riffles" the left-hand corner with his thumb, while asking the chooser of the card to think of it. The conjurer then "riffles" the end of the pack with his right thumb, and he knows that the pack will "break" at the faked card. This card will travel past the thumb, and the next card to it is the chosen card. The conjurer bends the pack slightly and gets a glimpse of it.

A second secret is a faked card made up in such a way that the whole pack, with the faked card in it, can be handed out to anyone to shuffle without the slightest fear of the discovery that one of the cards has been tampered with.

The faked card is easily made. The white edge of a card is first trimmed away, and the centre which is left is gummed on to the centre of another card. Thus the faked card will be slightly thicker in the centre than any other card, and the chosen card, replaced upon it, can be discovered quite easily by running the thumb along either end of the pack.

This secret also affords an excellent method of doing the blindfold trick. The conjurer can have the cards replaced on the faked card, and the pack immediately squared up. If he pleases, he can shuffle the cards, so long as he takes care not to disturb those immediately above the faked card. (If only one card has been chosen, either when this or the other faked card is used, there is little fear of the two cards being disturbed by an ordinary shuffle.) Having had the cards squared up, and having shown, after the shuffle, that the cards chosen are neither at the top nor at the bottom of the pack, the conjurer asks someone to blindfold him, and as he is not dependent upon the slightest speck of light for accomplishing the trick, he can even have his eyes covered with pads of cotton-wool before the handkerchief is placed over his eyes. He takes a small knife in his hand and spreads out the pack on the table.

The chosen cards are above the faked card. The position of the faked card is discovered by the touch of the fingers, and the cards immediately above it are pulled out to the edge of the table. The rest requires no explanation.

With regard to the use of the first faked pack, I may say that this gives anyone an easy way of producing any chosen cards from the pocket after the chosen cards have been returned to the pack, the pack has been returned to the conjurer and placed in his pocket. He can shuffle the pack casually before putting it in his pocket, and then asks the choosers of the cards if their cards are at the top or bottom of the pack. When the pack is in his pocket the conjurer merely has to run his thumb along the end, and the cards above the faked card will be the chosen cards. He turns this portion of the pack over and produces them one by one, or, if he pleases, he can leave the chosen cards in his pocket after he has removed the first card, and offer the pack to anyone to shuffle, and then put it back in his pocket. When the last chosen card has been taken out of his pocket, the conjurer takes out all the cards except the faked card, and goes on to the next trick. The use of a faked card is then not suspected.

DISCOVERING A CHOSEN CARD

A few cards—about half the pack—are held out by the performer, and he asks someone to select a card, look at it and replace it. The conjurer immediately gives out the pack to be shuffled, and directly he takes it back again he is able to pick out the chosen card.

It will be understood, of course, that this is not a trick, but a method by which a trick can be performed. No conjurer would be content merely to find the card; he would want to produce it in an effective manner. This merely shows how the card is discovered under these conditions. There are countless ways of producing the chosen card afterwards.

The conjurer should take the pack of cards in his hand, and draw from it the ace, three, five, six, seven, eight and nine of spades, clubs and hearts.

It will be seen that the cards with the odd numbers can be arranged so that single pips on the cards point in one direction. The aces' pips are obvious. In the three, the centre pip gives the clue; the same with the five. In the seven and nine the single pip in the centre of the card gives the clue, and in the six and eight the two centre pips on either side give the clue.

Now arrange the cards so that the pips giving the clue point all in one direction. If one card is chosen, and while the chooser is looking at it, the conjurer quietly reverses the cards he holds. It will be obvious that when the conjurer looks at the cards again, after they have been shuffled by a member of the audience, he can easily pick out the chosen card, because the pip giving the clue will point in the opposite direction to that of all the "clue pips" in all other cards.

THE FOUR AGES

Effect.—The conjurer places the four aces, face upwards, in a row on the table. He then puts them back on top of the pack and makes a sharp clicking noise with the pack (technically known as a "riffle"). A man who has been asked to assist in the trick is then invited to say where the aces are. Having heard the noise of the "riffle," he will probably believe that the aces have been brought by sleight-of-hand to the middle of the pack, and will probably say so. If he does say so, the conjurer at once shows that the aces are still on the top of the pack. If, on the other hand, the man says that the cards are still on top of the pack, the conjurer quickly makes the pass and brings them to the middle and shows them there. Then he says he will begin the trick again, and once more he puts the aces down on the table, and then on the top of the pack. The same little piece of by-play is carried out, and the aces are put down on the table for the third time, and for the third time, also, put on the top of the pack. This time the conjurer does the latter part of the work very slowly, and then asks: "Now, you are quite convinced that the aces are on the top of the pack?" There can be no doubt about this, and the man questioned is sure to say "Yes." The conjurer says he will get on with the trick, and this time deals the four aces face downwards on the table and then deals three cards on each ace. The assistant is asked to choose two of the packets and then one of the packets, so that finally there is only one packet on the table. The conjurer announces that he will try and make the three aces which have been returned to the pack change places with the three indifferent cards which are on the top of the fourth ace on the table. He riffles the cards three times, and then turns over the four cards on the table. They are the four aces.

Explanation.—Before showing this trick the conjurer secretly places three indifferent cards in his right-hand trousers pocket. He is then ready to perform the trick. To make the "riffle," he holds the cards in the left hand with the first finger pressed against the back of them. By pressing on one corner of the pack with the thumb and releasing the cards in that corner quickly, the conjurer makes a snapping noise with them. After the performer has put the cards on the table he stands for a second with his hands in his trousers pocket. It is as well for him to take up this attitude, a perfectly natural one, all through the trick, because when he wants to make use of the three cards in his pocket no one is likely to suspect him of using his pockets for the purpose of the trick.

The first two attempts at hoodwinking the assistant in regard to the position of the aces are of no consequence. There is no trickery required beyond the making of the pass, and even that is not always necessary, because often the assistant will help the conjurer by affirming that the aces are in the centre of the pack or at the bottom, in which case all that the conjurer has to do is to turn up the aces on the top and show that they have not moved from that position.

At the third attempt, the aces are placed slowly on the top of the pack, and once more the conjurer puts his hands into his pockets as he stands with an expectant attitude, and says, "Now, you're quite convinced that the aces are there?" This time he quietly palms the three indifferent cards from his pocket and secretly places them, in the act of squaring up the pack, on to the top of the aces. He then deals out the four top cards which the audience believe to be the four aces. On No. 4 card he places the next three cards, which, unknown to the audience, are the four aces. Three cards are dealt on each of the three remaining cards.

Looking at the packets of four cards from left to right, the conjurer knows that he has to force his assistant to choose No. 4 packet, on the right. He begins by asking the assistant to choose two of the packets, and then proceeds to influence his choice (without it being known) by means of "heads I win, tails you lose" principle. If the person chooses the first two packets the conjurer immediately takes them away, leaving No. 3 and No. 4 on the table. If, on the other hand, the assistant chooses No. 3 and No. 4, the conjurer says, "Very well, we will use one of those. Please choose another." If the choice falls on No. 4, the conjurer makes a great hit by pointing out that the packet which the person has freely chosen himself shall be used in the trick. If the person chooses No. 3, the conjurer takes it away and says, "That leaves us with one packet left. You could have had this one taken away if you had liked, couldn't you?" The way in which No. 4 packet, containing the four aces, is forced on the person who thinks all the time he has a free choice in the matter will now be quite clear. The audience never know, until the choice is actually made, whether the conjurer is going to take the chosen packet away from the table or leave it there. The rest of the trick explains itself.

THE "SYMPATHETIC" CARDS

To perform this trick, a pack of thirty-two cards is used. On the top are four queens in the following order: heart, spade, diamond, club; the queen of clubs on top. Bring, by means of the "pass," the queen of clubs to the middle of the pack, and force it on somebody. Now place the pack on the table, divide it into two heaps and place the top half, on which the three queens are, at the right side of the bottom half. Ask another spectator to choose one of the two heaps. In case the heap is chosen on which are the three queens, the performer picks it up, places it in his left hand and palms with the right the three queens, and gives heap to spectator to hold. The performer picks up other heap and places the palmed cards on the top of it and places the heap in the left hand. Now he asks the person who keeps the other half to take at random three cards from it one by one without looking at them. The performer places them on the heap he has himself, and as soon as all three are placed on top he passes them to the bottom. The three queens will thus remain on the top. Place carefully on a tray or plate the three top cards and hand them to a third person with request to place his other hand on the three cards. (It will be understood that it would facilitate matters in case the first spectator had chosen the bottom on the left-hand heap.)

The performer now makes the following remarks: "Ladies and gentlemen, when doing magical experiments, I occasionally remark that some of them depend entirely on the sympathy existing between the ladies and gentlemen of the company. The same can be said of cards, and in some cases the success depends on this, which I will try to prove by a little experiment."

The three cards chosen "sympathise" not only amongst themselves, but also with the three cards selected by the first gentleman, so that when, for instance, the first person has selected a knave, ace, seven or ten, the cards selected by the second person ought to be the same. Addressing the first person, the performer requests him to be so kind as to tell which card he selected. Queen of clubs will, of course, be the answer. Request the person who has his hand lying on the three cards to be so kind as to tell you what they are. They will prove to be queens also.

Show the four queens, and place them under the other half of the pack, after which the remaining heap must be placed again at the top. Now take secretly from the "profonde" four cards, which are prepared in such a way that on one side they show the four queens and the other side they show four spot cards. Place them secretly under the real four queens, picture side downwards. Seem to change your mind, and place the four bottom cards in a row on the table, with the queen side exposed. Request somebody to choose any one of the four queens, not to touch it, but by calling it out. By the way, the four queens at the bottom of the pack must lie in the same order as the four prepared queens lying on the table. Suppose the queen of hearts is chosen. The performer at once passes to the top of the pack the four bottom cards, and quickly slips the queen of hearts to the bottom of the three other queens lying at the top of pack. After this is done, place on each queen lying on the table three ordinary cards, taken one by one from the bottom of the pack. Place them face downwards and be careful that they cover the queens entirely. There are now lying on the table four heaps, each of four cards. Pick up the heap in which is the chosen queen of hearts, change this heap quietly with the four queens lying on top of pack, and, advancing to the person who selected the queen of hearts, give to him, the four queens to hold. To the spectators, it will appear that they are the four cards taken from the table, namely the queen of hearts, with three other cards on top. Be careful that only the backs of the cards are visible. Now touch with your wand three heaps on the table, and also the heap kept by the spectator. Pick up separately each heap from the table, turn them around, spread them out and show that the queens have departed. Request spectator to show his card, and the audience will see the four queens.

THE CIGARETTE TRICK

A card is selected from the pack, torn in pieces, one piece given back for the purpose of identifying the card later. A piece of paper is shown to the audience and the paper is folded into a square to resemble an envelope. The pieces of card are dropped into the paper, and all sides folded down, the paper being given to one of the company to hold. The pistol is fired, the paper torn open, and the card is found restored, except the small piece which was given back to the company. The card and the small piece are placed in a card-box. You tell the audience that you are going to restore the card to its original condition. As it will take a few seconds to go through the process, if the company do not mind, you will "enjoy a smoke" while waiting. Borrow a cigarette, attempt to light it, say it is strange it will not light; then tear it open, and instead of tobacco, the chosen card is inside, the box being opened is found empty.

The card is forced; the supposed piece of paper is really two pieces pasted together, with a duplicate of chosen card, corner torn off, in centre. The envelope being formed round the card, when torn open it is slit along the front edge with a penknife. The cigarette is changed for a faked one, and the card rolled up and enclosed in cigarette paper. The card box is normal.

THE MEXICAN TURN OVER

Effect.—The queen and two other cards are placed in a row on the table, and the performer moving them about as though he would confuse his audience, asks someone to "find the lady." The person choosing is told at once that he is wrong. The conjurer picks up one of the other cards and slipping it under the chosen card, turns it over and shows that it is not the queen. He then turns over the other card in the same way, and finally throws the card he is holding on the table.

Explanation.—Let us suppose that the person who is asked to "find the lady." points to the card which the conjurer knows is the queen. He picks up one of the other cards, face downwards, and slips it under the queen and a little in advance of it so that the top of the card in his hand is about half an inch beyond the top of the queen on the table. The card in the hand is held at the tips of the first finger and thumb. When this card is well underneath the queen, the conjurer moves his thumb to the corner of the queen card, and thus holds that card face downwards while he turns over the other card with the tip of his first finger. The effect to the audience is that the conjurer merely turned over one card with another.

The reason for turning over the other card on the table is this: after the conjurer has turned over the first card, he is holding the queen in his hand. By turning over the second card and using this queen, he is able to show that it was the second card that was the queen. If he merely showed that the card in his hand was the queen the audience might suspect some kind of change, although if the trick is done neatly and quickly it is quite impossible for anyone to detect it.

THE MISSING CARD

Effect.—A card having been chosen and returned to the pack the conjurer shuffles the cards, removes three, and places them on the table. He announces that the chosen card is one of the three and says that by means of his own will power he will cause the person who drew the card to touch the actual card that he chose. The person is invited to touch one of the three cards. He does so. The card is turned over and is not the chosen card. The conjurer then pretends that he has made a mistake and asks the person to look at the other two cards on the table. Neither of them is the chosen card. "Some mistake," says the conjurer, looking through the pack. "By the way, which card did you take? The six of clubs (or whatever card is named). I'm sorry, but I think you have made a mistake; there is no such card here." He then runs through the pack and shows that the six of clubs is undoubtedly missing. A search is made for the the card and eventually the person who chose it is asked to get up, when the audience see that he has been sitting on the card all the time.

Explanation.—After the card is returned and brought to the top of the pack the conjurer takes any three cards and places them on the table well away from the person assisting him so that when the person is asked to touch one of the cards he has to rise from his chair to do so. The conjurer stands close to him while he gets up and holds the pack in his right hand. When the person is well away from his chair and while all eyes are on the cards on the table the conjurer quietly pushes off the top card with his right thumb, so that when the person sits down again he covers the card.

THE RISING CARD

A large frame is standing on the table. At the base of the frame is a receptacle for holding a pack of cards, and at the top of the frame is a tiny ornamental arch. Having had a card chosen by the audience and returned to the pack, the conjurer hands the pack to another member of the audience with a request that he will shuffle it thoroughly. The conjurer then places the pack in the receptacle and asks what card was chosen. Suppose it was the two of hearts. Commanding the card to show itself, the conjurer makes some passes towards the frame, and the card rises slowly to the top of the ornamental arch above the frame.

Explanation.—The card is forced. The houlette or receptacle is provided with an extra space at the back, and in this is placed a card similar to the one which is to be forced. This card has a thread attached to it. The thread is drawn up to the arch, passed through a little hole there, and then brought down and fastened to a little weight concealed in one of the sides of the frame. This weight rests on the top of some sand in the sides of the frame. When the conjurer wishes the card to rise he releases a little catch at the bottom of the side of the frame and the sand runs into the bottom of the frame. This action causes the little weight to drop down into the side of the frame, and in doing this it naturally draws down the thread and so causes the card to rise. The conjurer stands away from the apparatus while the card is rising, to prove that he is "not operating the trick in any way."

THE MYSTIC CARD-BOX

The performer hands out a small flat box for inspection. Someone in the audience is invited to take any card from a pack and place it in the box. The conjurer, holding the box to his forehead, immediately names the card in the box.

Here is the explanation. One of the screws at the back of the box is a dummy. In holding up the box the conjurer pulls out this dummy nail a little way. This enables the conjurer to slide the front panel a little to one side with his thumb. At the lower right-hand corner there is a small hole in the panel, and through this the conjurer is able to read the index corner of the card. The frame can be immediately restored to its original condition and handed out for inspection.

THE WATCH AND THE CARD

Someone in the audience is invited to shuffle the pack, take a card, replace it in the pack, and shuffle the pack again. The conjurer wraps the pack in a handkerchief and places it on the table. He then takes out his watch and asks someone to tell him the time; he shows that person that his watch is in good going order and is very nearly "on time." The watch is placed on the covered pack of cards.

The conjurer tells his audience that the watch will help him in the trick by telling him what card was taken.

He immediately names the card and then shows the audience how he gained the information from the watch. The watch is of an unusual kind; the usual figures from the face have vanished and their places have been taken by some miniature cards. The hand of the watch is pointing to a card similar to that which was chosen.

The climax of the trick is reached when the conjurer uncovers the pack, and, riffling it, shows that the chosen card has disappeared from the pack.

After a member of the audience has shuffled the pack the conjurer forces a card; this card is slightly shorter than the remaining cards in the pack. After the card is returned to the pack, anyone may shuffle the cards.

The object of the conjurer in asking the time is merely to give him a chance of showing his watch in a natural way. If he took the watch from his pocket and called attention to the fact that he was going to use the watch in the trick, somebody would probably want to look too closely at the watch. The watch is really only a dummy with small cards and a hand on the face. Over the face of the watch there is a false dial, similar to that of an ordinary watch. After the conjurer has called attention to the watch, he places it on the covered pack of cards and in doing so palms off the false dial which is attached to the body of the watch by means of a small bayonet catch. A slight turn releases the dial and the watch is placed on the packet.

As the forced card was slightly shorter than the rest of the cards there is no difficulty in causing it to vanish when the cards are riffled, for its face cannot be seen when the cards are "sprung" by the riffle.

THINK OF A CARD

Having invited someone to shuffle the pack the conjurer deals off three cards, asks the person assisting to think of one of them and not to give him any clue as to the card chosen.

The performer then puts the three cards in his pocket and repeats his request to his assistant to think intently of the chosen card. The conjurer takes two of the cards from his pocket and throws them on the table. He then asks his assistant to name the card of which he is thinking, and immediately takes that card from his pocket, thus showing that he had "read" the person's thoughts.

The explanation is as follows. The conjurer prepares for the trick by slipping two cards into his pocket; these cards can be hidden by means of the old trick of pushing them to the top of the pocket. No two pockets are quite alike and it may be necessary to bend the cards in order to fix them in their right position. When he deals the cards on the table the conjurer memorises them, or, alternatively, he can see that the cards are arranged in numerical order; he need not trouble to remember the suits.

With the order of the three cards clearly fixed in his mind, the conjurer puts them in his pocket, and after some little pretence at thought reading takes from his pocket the two cards which he hid in his pocket before the beginning of the trick. It is not advisable to show the faces of these cards, because it is just possible that the assistant may have remembered all three cards which were shown to him, and in that case he would at once notice that the conjurer was using two extra cards.

Having thrown the two cards on the table the conjurer asks his assistant to name the card of which he has been thinking.

The conjurer, remembering the order of the three cards in his pocket, has no difficulty in drawing the particular card required from his pocket.

CARDS, COINS, AND GLASS

The performer introduces an ordinary pack of playing cards and a glass tumbler; they may be examined if necessary. He then borrows a number of coins (say three). The tumbler is placed on the table, cards on top of it, and, at the command of the conjurer, the coins leave his hand, and are distinctly seen and heard to fall into the tumbler.

A fake, made as follows, is needed. Cut an ordinary playing card in two. Take one half and paint black both sides. Glue a piece of black linen on one side at about half an inch from the end (oblong). Attach fake to long thread with loop at end and fasten to vest button, put wand under left arm, take coins in left hand, stand away the length of the thread, make pass from left to right, take wand in right hand. Give thread a downward blow with wand, when the fake flies out and coins fall into the glass. Now break thread off vest button, and let it fall on carpet.

Anyone can then take up coins, cards and glass for examination. When performing this trick, stand well behind the table.

FIVE CARDS TO VANISH AND REAPPEAR

Effect.—One card is picked up by the magician, who makes it disappear. He picks up another card with his left hand, places it in the right hand and makes that one disappear. He continues in the same way with five cards. Then, raising his right hand in the air, with a quick movement, he brings the cards back one at a time.

Explanation.—The effect is produced by what is known as the "back and front palm." The first card is held in the centre of one end between the second finger and thumb of the right hand. The conjurer waves his hand up and down, and that movement covers the movements of the fingers which are necessary to get the card to the back of the hand, where it is concealed.

These are the movements of the fingers: the card is held between the tips of the second finger and thumb. Now the little finger and first finger come up at the sides of the card. The second finger is bent towards the palm, and the thumb is released while the card is gripped between the first and second fingers and little and third fingers. To make the card disappear all that is now necessary is to straighten the hand.

To "back palm" the other cards, each is brought up by the left hand to the right, and dealt with in the same manner, each card sliding on to those at the back of the hand.

To cause the reappearance of the cards one at a time, the conjurer proceeds in the following manner: turning his hand round from the wrist and in such a way that the cards cannot be seen by the audience (the exact angle at which the hand should be held can be determined by doing the trick before a looking-glass), the conjurer bends his fingers and then slides the top card of the packet upwards with his thumb; the little finger releases it, but grips the remaining cards.

The conjurer then extends his first finger and slides it under the card and straightens his hand. This brings one card to view, and keeps the remainder at the back of the hand. The process is repeated to cause the reappearance of the other cards.

If the conjurer pleases he can show that the cards have completely disappeared even when they are held by his right hand; that is to say, he shows both the back and the front of his hand. Suppose that the cards have been brought to the back in the way described. The conjurer bends his fingers, extends the second finger and with it pushes the cards from the top into the hand. The cards are not palmed in the usual way but are held by the edges between the first and second fingers and third and little fingers. They are then in readiness to be back palmed again.

One card is manipulated very easily in this way. Instead of using the second finger to push the card down into the hand, the magician drags the card down quickly by using his thumb. Simultaneously the hand is turned over, and the audience can see that there is no card at the back of the hand.

DIMINISHING CARDS

The trick of making cards appear to diminish requires considerable skill. Here is the description and explanation:

The packs of cards you deal with are tied up with a thread. At the back of each pack there is a spring slip, into which the packet of the next size smaller is inserted. Having got the packs palmed in his left hand the conjurer volunteers to show the audience how it is all done.

He picks up a few cards, places his two hands together and exhibits the largest of the small packs and at the same time palms the big cards which he had picked up. With the excuse of showing how the cards have shrunk, the conjurer now picks up some more big cards with his right hand, and in returning them to the table returns the palmed cards with them. The audience now see the face of the top lot of cards reduced to the size of Patience cards. The conjurer now pretends to make these smaller, but he really pushes them down a little lower in his hands. Picking up a card from the table to show how small the cards are getting he continues the process, and puts the card down again. This card has a flap at the back. When the card is on the table it is flat, but when it is held with its face towards the audience the flap opens, leaving a little pocket, in which the first packet of small diminishing cards is dropped. The front card of the next size is a flap card, which can be opened to the size of a Patience card. The process is repeated; each time the conjurer picks up a card to show how small the cards are getting. By means of the flap cards all palming of small packets is done away with.

THE SWINDLE TRICK

The conjurer has a card selected and returned to the pack and the pack shuffled. The cards are strewn about the table. The conjurer picks up the cards one at a time, turns each one over, looks at it, looks at the spectator who drew the card as though he would read his thoughts and then puts the card into his left hand.

He continues to do this until he has a number of cards in his hand, each one of which the spectator has seen. Among them is the card that the Spectator originally drew and returned to the pack. Therefore, when the conjurer says: "The next card I turn over will be yours," the spectator, having seen that the card he chose has already been picked up and put in the conjurer's hand, will certainly say, "You're wrong." "Impossible," says the conjurer, "the next card I turn over will be yours." "But you've passed it," says the victim. "You're wrong," says the conjurer, and then takes a card from those in his hand—not one on the table, as the spectator thought—turns it over, and it is, of course, the selected card.

This is the way it is done. When the card is returned to the pack the conjurer holds his fingers under the pack and quietly bends a corner of the card. He is thus able to tell from feeling the card when he picks up the chosen one, and in putting it into his left hand he keeps his little finger on top of it. He takes care, of course, that the spectator gets a good view of this card, and then goes on picking up cards and looking at each one before he brings the trick to its conclusion.

THE MYSTERIOUS COUPLE

Two cards are freely chosen and returned to the pack. The conjurer shuffles the pack, and, holding it in the left hand with the bottom card only visible, asks the first chooser if that was his card. The reply is negative. The conjurer deals this bottom card on the table, and, going to the second chooser, asks if the bottom card is his card. Again the reply is "No." From this point the patter is:

"My trick is fairly simple. I will first ask what were the chosen cards—the king of hearts and the three of diamonds. (They may, of course, be any other cards.) Very well. I think you all saw me place the two bottom cards of the pack—the five of diamonds and the ten of clubs (if those were the cards used)—on the table. What I propose to do is to ask the cards on the table to change places with those cards which were chosen. When you heard that little click (made by the riffle) the change took place, and if you now look at the cards you will see that the five of diamonds and the ten of clubs which I dealt on the table have returned to the pack and that the chosen cards—the king of hearts and three of diamonds—are on the table. There they are."

This little piece of magic is brought about by means of half a card, or rather the halves of two cards, pasted together back to back. The conjurer hides this fake under the other cards when he has the two cards chosen. He brings the two chosen cards to the bottom of the pack, and keeps the faked card over one end. In holding up the pack for the first man to see, he keeps his hand in such a position that only the half-card is seen, and the junction between that and the real bottom card is hidden by the hand. When he turns the pack face downwards, and apparently draws out the card which has been shown to the member of the audience, the conjurer keeps hold of the faked card and draws out the bottom card, which is one of the two chosen cards.

The conjurer then turns the faked card over and repeats the process, and gets rid of the faked card in any way he pleases. The only part of the trick in which special care should be taken is in not allowing the two choosers of cards to take cards similar to those on the two sides of the faked card. It is, however, a comparatively simple matter to have these two cards and the faked half-card at the bottom of the pack before the commencement of the trick, and then there is no chance of a mishap.

BLINDFOLDING THE CARDS

Effect.—The conjurer comes forward with three handkerchiefs, which he says he is going to use for the purpose of "blindfolding the cards." He has the pack divided in halves. The person doing this is then invited to divide either half into three small heaps, and to wrap each heap in a handkerchief so that the cards may be blindfolded. The person is then asked to choose one of the heaps. The conjurer takes this heap and holds it close to his forehead. He then calls out the names of several cards, and when the handkerchief is taken away the audience see that the cards named by the conjurer were those in the handkerchief.

Explanation.—A prearranged pack is used. When the person who has been helping the conjurer indicates which heap is to be used in the trick the conjurer says, "Very well, we shall not want these," and puts the other heaps on one side, but in doing this he secretly stretches the handkerchief, which should be a fine one, over the bottom card of the heap above the one chosen and sees the card through the handkerchief. He then takes up the chosen heap and holds it to his forehead. In doing this he stretches the handkerchief, sees the bottom card and, therefore, knowing the order of the cards, he can name those in the handkerchief, because knowing the bottom card of the next heap he is able to tell the top card of those he is holding.

CARDS AND A FAN

Effect.—A spectator is asked to assist by freely choosing a card and writing upon it his initials. The card is placed in an envelope, which is closed and given to another member of the audience. The first assistant is now requested to shuffle the pack and fan it. The performer draws a card from fan, calls its name, and, initialling it, puts it in his pocket. These two cards change places and can be immediately shown and initials verified.

Method.—The only preparation necessary is to reverse the two bottom cards of the pack and initial the last one. The pack is false-shuffled, care being taken to keep reversed cards out of sight. The spectator freely chooses a card, and the performer, by fanning pack from top to centre, will prevent the bottom cards being observed. The chosen card is initialled, returned to top of pack, and is reversed before placing on the table. The performer lifts oft top card, which is now really bottom card with his own initials, and lays it face down on table. He now lifts up pack and envelope and gives the latter for examination, meanwhile palming the original top card to trousers pocket. The card on the table is placed in an envelope. The remaining reversed card is now altered to agree with rest of pack, which is given to a spectator, who is asked to shuffle and fan. The performer picks a card, does not show it, but calls the name of the card he prepared beforehand. A pretence is made of initialling it. Finally it is placed on "top" of trousers pocket. Cards may now be commanded to change places, and pocket, by aid of "top" principle, may be shown empty after spectator's card is removed.

(This trick was devised by Margaret Mackey.)

CARDS RISING FROM THE POCKET

Effect.—Three cards are selected and returned to the pack, which is then shuffled and placed in the outside breast pocket of the conjurer's coat. The conjurer asks the choosers of the three cards to name them and he calls upon them to come out of his pocket; the cards obey him, and rise, one at a time, from the pocket.

Explanation.—The three cards are forced, therefore, after they are returned to the pack anyone is at liberty to shuffle the pack. Inside the pocket there is a little "buckram" partition with three duplicate cards threaded in the usual way. The end of the thread is passed out through the back of the coat and is attached to a spring ratchet winder sewn in the lining of the coat. To cause the cards to rise the conjurer stands, in a natural position, with his left hand on hip and presses on a little knob on the winder; this releases the spring and winds up the thread, causing the first card to rise. The movement is repeated for the other two cards. This trick and the following one is the work of Elbert M. Morey.

THE SUSPENDED CARDS

Effect.—Three cards are chosen, and returned to the pack. The conjurer, standing in front of a small black velvet screen, throws the pack up in the air. The three chosen cards remain suspended in the air, and the conjurer takes them and hands them out for inspection.

Explanation.—The screen is fitted with three short rods

with a card concealed by means of black velvet at the end of each rod. The three cards, duplicates of the three which are forced on three members of the audience, are enclosed in little black velvet bags. These three rods work on three weak spring hinges, and when the cards are to be made to appear a pull at the back of the screen raises the three rods and thus brings the cards into view; as the rods are covered with black velvet the cards appear to be suspended in mid-air.

HERSCHELL'S ENVELOPES AND CARDS

The following trick was invented by the late Dr. Herschell. Two cards, both of which may be examined before and after the trick, are placed respectively into two envelopes, each of which is provided with a round hole in the centre. By this provision, when cards are placed into envelopes, their centre pips (both cards being nines) are visible to the last moment. In spite of the apparent fairness of the preliminaries, the two cards manage to change places, the red taking the place of the black and vice versa.

Only two cards are used, and neither has any preparation in connection with it. Not so the envelopes. The front of each is made double to conceal a lever, the long arm of which carries a square piece of card on which is painted the pip of a card. One envelope has a club pip concealed, the other a heart.

The short arms projecting beyond corners of the envelope, a very slight pressure serves to bring the respective pips into view through the holes. Little more needs to be explained. The nine of hearts goes into the envelope containing the club lever; the nine of clubs goes into the one containing the heart lever. The envelopes are now placed on top of each other, and the levers moved to bring the faked pips into view. Whilst showing two tumblers, against which the envelopes are eventually lodged, the audience naturally fail to remember the positions of the respective cards. Each envelope is now shown and careful attention drawn to the respective positions of the cards. In turning the envelopes round so that the holes are away from the audience, the levers are pushed aside, so that the cards a few seconds later appear to have changed their positions.

THE HERSCHELL CARD-STABBING TRICK

A selected card is revealed on the point of a dagger, although the spread pack is covered with a piece of newspaper.

The trick is simple, a faked sheet of newspaper being responsible for practically the whole mystery. A pocket made in a sheet of newspaper conceals a duplicate of the card, which is, of course, forced on a spectator. Let us imagine that the ace of spades is forced. A duplicate of this is "loaded" into the pocket of the paper, and if the paper is neatly faked there is no chance of its presence being detected. So soon as the card is returned to the pack, it is brought to top and palmed away. Ample opportunity for the necessary manipulation is afforded while a bandage for the eyes is examined.

The piercing of the duplicate with the dagger in these circumstances is not a difficult matter, as the performer knows the exact position of the pocket and stabs accordingly.

THE "MIRACLE."

A pack of cards in a case is handed to the audience by the conjurer, who asks someone to take out the cards, shuffle them, and select one card. The remainder of the pack is returned to the case, which is handed back to the conjurer, who slips it into his trousers pocket.

The person holding the card is asked to show it to several other members of the audience, and so that he shall not catch a glimpse of the card the conjurer turns his back on the audience for a moment. While he is in that position, the conjurer takes the case from his pocket and, holding it behind his back, asks the holder of the card to put it back in the pack, close the case, and put a rubber band round it. The performer turns round and immediately names the chosen card.

This is how it is done! The performer is provided with two

packs of cards and two cases just alike. One pack is prepared by having an index corner of each card cut out of it. One case has a little piece cut out of the bottom right-hand corner. The space is equal in size to the index corner of a card. The prepared pack is placed in this case and just before he is going to do the trick the conjurer puts the case in his pocket.

The working of the trick, the invention of Hans Trunk, will now be clear. After the card has been chosen the conjurer puts the prepared case, with the case with the prepared cards in it, into his trousers pocket. He eventually takes out the prepared case and holding it behind him with the cut-out corner next to his body, invites the spectator to return his card to the case. Directly the performer brings the case in front of him he is able to see the index corner of the selected card.

THE THREE HEAPS

Effect.—The spectator, having cut the pack into three heaps, is asked if he has cut them exactly where he pleased. The answer is, of course, "Yes." The conjurer says, "How curious that you should have cut them just where I wished—at the——" and names the top card of each heap.

Explanation.—The conjurer gets a glimpse of the bottom card and brings this to the top by a shuffle. To do this the conjurer picks up the cards in his right hand and turns them over so that the bottom card is facing him. In drawing off some cards with the left hand at the beginning of the shuffle the conjurer puts his thumb on this card and brings it singly into his left hand. The other cards may be fairly shuffled on the top, and then, when the pack is turned over, the card which was formerly at the bottom is now at the top. The spectator cuts the pack into three heaps. In naming the cards at the top of the three heaps the conjurer first names the card he knows is the top card of the pack, but he takes up the card of the middle heap and says "Right," as though he had actually drawn the card he named. He names this first card when he takes up the card of the lowest heap, and names this second card when he takes up the top card of the last heap. That card, being the original top card of the pack, is the card he named in the first place. Thus he has named all three cards.

THE FRIENDLY CARDS

Effect.—The conjurer asks a member of the audience to choose a card and replace it in the pack. He then asks another spectator to think of any card in the pack. This being done the conjurer deals the cards from the bottom of the pack until he comes to the card of which the spectator is thinking. The next card he deals is the one which has been taken from and returned to the pack. In some way the two cards have shown themselves "friendly" and have appeared together.

Explanation.—There is no pretence about the spectator thinking of a card. The conjurer asks him what card he is going to think of. He has previously had the first card returned to the pack, and by bringing it to the bottom has it in readiness for the completion of his trick. He holds the pack in his left hand with the fingers on the bottom card. By using his third finger he draws this card back and deals out the other cards until he comes to the one which was thought of. The next card he takes out is the card chosen and replaced in the pack because he has had that card drawn back at the bottom of the pack all the time.

FLIGHT

Effect.—The conjurer has a card selected and placed back in the pack. He asks the chooser to name any person in the room and announces that he will try and make the selected card fly invisibly across the room and into that person's pocket. Having pronounced a "magical password," the conjurer announces that the card has flown from the pack, but when the person chosen to receive it looks into his pocket the card is not there. The conjurer expresses surprise at this and asks the chooser of the card what card it was what he took from the pack. When he is told the name of the card the conjurer says that it is a special favourite of his, and that therefore the card never goes to a stranger, but always flies into his own pocket. He invites anyone to feel in his inside coat pocket, and when this is done the missing card is found there.

Explanation.—The conjurer has to force a card, the duplicate of which is already in his coat pocket. The chosen card is put back into the pack and, if the conjurer wishes to make the trick more effective, he brings it to the top by means of the pass and palms it off. He can either drop it behind a handkerchief on the table or slip it into his trousers pocket. The trick is then done. The surprise of the trick lies in the fact that the conjurer never goes to the pocket from which the card is subsequently taken.

A CARD TRAVELS INVISIBLY

Effect.—The conjurer takes a card from the top of the pack and causes it to disappear for a second. He "finds" it again, and places it in the other hand. Then the card travels backwards and forwards from one hand to the other. It can be passed through the knees or through the body.

Explanation.—The conjurer has two cards alike on top of the pack. He takes these off and shows them as one card. Back palming these he reproduces one of the cards and leaves the other at the back of his hand. He takes the visible one with his left hand and back palms it, at the same time causing the one at the back of the right hand to appear in that hand. He continues the movements, back palming with one hand and causing the card in the other hand to appear. Then he holds the hands close to the body and makes the cards apparently travel right through the body. He can do the same thing by bending down and holding his hands close at the sides of the knees (the legs being close together) so that the card appears to travel through the legs. The cards are then put together as one card and replaced on the pack.

Made in the USA
Coppell, TX
09 January 2021